National Parks

Cuyahoga Valley

JOANNE MATTERN

Children's Press®
An Imprint of Scholastic Inc.

Content Consultant
James Gramann, PhD
Professor Emeritus, Department of Recreation, Park and Tourism Sciences
Texas A&M University, College Station, Texas

Library of Congress Cataloging-in-Publication Data
Names: Mattern, Joanne, 1963– author.
Title: Cuyahoga Valley / by Joanne Mattern.
Description: New York, NY : Children's Press, an imprint of Scholastic Inc., 2018. | Series: A true
    book | Includes bibliographical references and index.
Identifiers: LCCN 2018002254 | ISBN 9780531175934 (library binding) | ISBN 9780531189986 (pbk.)
Subjects: LCSH: Cuyahoga Valley National Park (Ohio)—Juvenile literature.
Classification: LCC F497.C95 M365 2018 | DDC 977.1/31—dc23
LC record available at https://lccn.loc.gov/2018002254

All rights reserved. Published in 2019 by Children's Press, an imprint of Scholastic Inc.
Printed in Heshan, China 62

SCHOLASTIC, CHILDREN'S PRESS, A TRUE BOOK™, and associated logos are trademarks and/or
registered trademarks of Scholastic Inc.

Scholastic Inc., 557 Broadway, New York, NY 10012

1 2 3 4 5 6 7 8 9 10 R 28 27 26 25 24 23 22 21 20 19

**Front cover (main): A train passes under
a bridge in the Cuyahoga Valley**
Front cover (inset): Great blue heron
Back cover: Brandywine Falls

Find the Truth!

Everything you are about to read is true *except* for one of the sentences on this page.

Which one is **TRUE**?

T or F The great blue heron disappeared from the park in the 1980s.

T or F Cuyahoga Valley was once at the bottom of the sea.

Find the answers in this book.

3

Contents

1 Shaped by the Past

What did the Cuyahoga Valley
look like long ago?.........................7

2 Valley Geography

How did water shape the park? 15

3 Animals of the Valley

What kinds of wildlife live in the park?..........21

THE **BIG** TRUTH!

National Parks Field Guide: Cuyahoga Valley

How can visitors identify some
of the park's animals?................28

Raccoon

Cuyahoga Valley Scenic Railroad

4 An Abundance of Plants

What plants grow in Cuyahoga Valley National Park? 31

5 Facing the Future

What problems does Cuyahoga Valley face? 37

Map Mystery 40
Be an Animal Tracker! 42
True Statistics 44
Resources 45
Important Words 46
Index 47
About the Author 48

Bald eagle

There are two ways to pronounce Cuyahoga: "kye-uh-HOH-guh" and "kye-uh-HAW-guh."

Brandywine Falls is one of Cuyahoga Valley's most popular places to visit.

CHAPTER 1

Shaped by the Past

Where can you hike in the woods, bike along a **canal**, and ride a historic railroad? In the only national park in Ohio: Cuyahoga Valley.

   Millions of years ago, ancient seas covered the area that is now Cuyahoga Valley National Park. Dirt washed into the sea. It built up into layers of **sediment**. In time, the sediment hardened into rock called shale. The shale now found in the park is filled with **fossils** of the sea animals that once lived there.

Cuyahoga Valley National Park

Glaciers and a River

About two million years ago, an Ice Age began. Huge **glaciers** moved across what is now Ohio. They carved the rock like bulldozers cutting up fields. New valleys took shape. Existing valleys were filled in with rocks the glaciers pushed aside.

That Ice Age ended about 10,000 years ago. The glaciers disappeared. A river began to flow. Over time, the Cuyahoga River shaped the landscape. The Cuyahoga Valley was born.

A Timeline of Cuyahoga Valley National Park

11,000 BCE

Humans first arrive in the Cuyahoga Valley, hunting saber-toothed cats and other now-extinct animals.

1700s CE

European fur trappers and settlers come to the area.

1795

The Treaty of Greenville forces most Native Americans from land east of the Cuyahoga River.

Native Americans in the Valley

The first people in the Cuyahoga Valley arrived about 13,000 years ago. They were hunter-gatherers. Many centuries later, Native American cultures such as the Hopewell settled in the area. They named the river *Cuyahoga*, or "crooked river."

The inhabitants caught fish in the river and ate plants that grew along its banks. They also hunted in the nearby woods. In fields, they planted melons, corn, squash, beans, and apples.

1832
The Ohio and Erie Canal is completed and open to boat traffic.

1929
Virginia Kendall Park is created.

1974
President Gerald Ford signs the bill creating a National Recreation Area.

2000
The area becomes Cuyahoga Valley National Park.

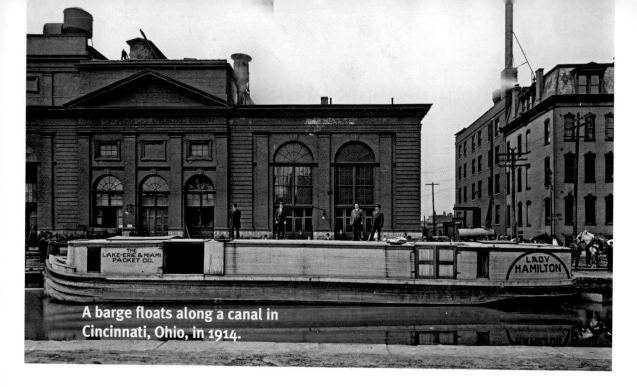

A barge floats along a canal in Cincinnati, Ohio, in 1914.

Europeans Arrive

In time, the Cuyahoga River attracted fur traders from Europe and the eastern United States. They trapped beavers, muskrats, and other animals, and then sold their furs.

By 1812, white traders, farmers, and other settlers had pushed Native Americans off the land. The new settlers also built the Ohio and Erie Canal to link the Cuyahoga River to Lake Erie.

New Communities

The settlers also used the Cuyahoga River as a power source, building **mills** along the river. As businesses grew, more people moved in. Soon the valley was filled with towns.

Moses and Polly Gleeson were two of the new settlers. They bought a building along the Ohio and Erie Canal in 1837. Over time they added to the building, serving canal travelers with a store, a restaurant, and more. Today, that building is the park's Canal Exploration Center.

Trains once brought coal and travelers to the Cuyahoga Valley and nearby cities. Today, the train gives tourists a scenic view of the park.

Creating the Park

Over the years, the valley grew crowded. Many people missed the quiet beauty of the woods and the river. They wanted to protect a natural landscape where people could escape city life.

In 1929, Agnes Kendall, the wealthy widow of an Ohio businessman, donated land to create a park. She named it the Virginia Kendall Park after her husband's mother. In 1974, the U.S. Congress turned the park and nearby land into the Cuyahoga Valley National Recreation Area. A recreation area focuses on offering people a place to have fun in nature. But residents wanted stronger protection for the land. In 2000, the area became a national park. This made the park's focus protecting the land and its wildlife.

National Park Fact File

A national park is land that is protected by the federal government. It is a place of importance to the United States because of its beauty, history, or value to scientists. The U.S. Congress creates a national park by passing a law. Here are some key facts about Cuyahoga Valley National Park.

Cuyahoga Valley National Park	
Location	Northeastern Ohio
Year established	2000
Size	51 square miles (132 sq km)
Average number of visitors each year	2.2 million
Height of tallest waterfall	65 feet (20 meters), Brandywine Falls
Famous features	Historic buildings, Beaver Marsh, Ritchie Ledges, Ohio and Erie Canal

The park includes five major trails for biking.

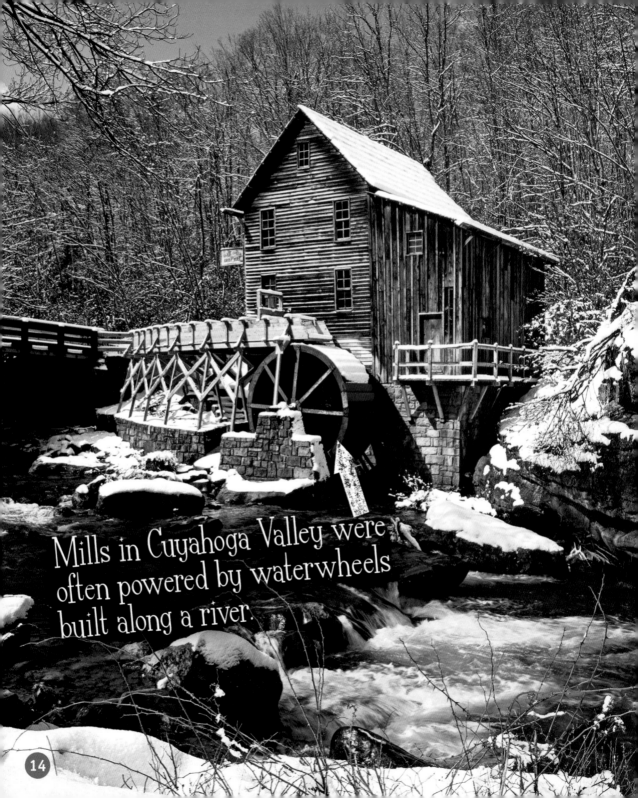

Mills in Cuyahoga Valley were often powered by waterwheels built along a river.

CHAPTER 2

Valley Geography

Cuyahoga Valley has countless natural features to enjoy. The park also has a surprising number of human-made sites, including more than 100 ponds and lakes! There are also examples of the industry that settlers brought to the area, from historic mills to the mighty Ohio and Erie Canal.

Visitors to Cuyahoga can follow old railroad tracks and even bike or hike along towpaths where animals pulled barges along the canal. This park offers something for everyone.

The Cuyahoga Valley Scenic Railroad follows the basic path of the Cuyahoga River.

A Mighty River

The Cuyahoga River flows about 100 miles (161 kilometers) in a U-shape through northeastern Ohio. About 22 miles (35 km) of it are in the park. Here fish, frogs, and insects thrive. Reptiles, mammals, and birds feed on these creatures that live in the water.

Many streams and creeks join the river in the park. Some only flow after heavy rains or snowmelt. Others are much larger. The largest is Tinkers Creek at 28 miles (45 km) long.

Other Waters

The spectacular Brandywine Falls is part of Brandywine Creek. This 65-foot (20 m) waterfall is the tallest in the park. Moisture in the air around the falls allows moss to grow on nearby rocks and trees.

Elsewhere in the park, beavers created a pond at Beaver Marsh when they built a dam. A marsh is a kind of **wetlands** habitat. The ground around the pond is wet all year. Many plants thrive here, along with frogs, turtles, and numerous birds.

Clusters of lily pads cover sections of the water's surface at Beaver Marsh.

Moss grows on the high rock walls of the Ritchie Ledges.

Rocks and Caves

There are some amazing rock formations in the park. One of the most beautiful areas is the Ritchie Ledges. Glaciers shaped this region millions of years ago. Hikers who follow the Ledges Trail see towering sandstone cliffs. Enormous boulders lie on the ground. There is also a cave called the Ice Box Cave. But visitors are not allowed inside. This is to protect the many bats that make their home there.

The Krejci Dump

Just as human activity can damage and pollute natural landscapes, our actions can also create huge positive changes to an environment. Cuyahoga Valley provides a shining example of this. The Krejci (KRETCH-ee) Dump was once filled with barrels of toxic chemicals and piles of waste. In 1987, the U.S. Environmental Protection Agency started to clean up the dump.

The National Park Service took over the job in 1988. Workers removed all the trash and polluted soil, and over time the land returned to its natural state. The area is gradually becoming a healthy, beautiful wetland and meadow, enjoyed by thousands of visitors.

Dump site before restoration

Dump site today

CHAPTER 3

Animals of the Valley

Cuyahoga Valley National Park is home to a huge variety of animals. From rivers to woodlands, the park includes a range of ecosystems. Visitors can spot animals in the sky, the trees, and the rivers, caves, and lakes. Take a peek at any section of the park and you are bound to find wildlife!

Peregrine falcons can dive toward prey at up to 200 miles (320 km) per hour.

Mammals

There are 39 mammal species in the park. The largest mammal in the park is the white-tailed deer. Deer live throughout the park and feed themselves in the grassy fields and forests. Coyotes recently

made a comeback in the area after disappearing for many years. These predators eat smaller animals like chipmunks and squirrels. They also eat fruit, berries, nuts, and seeds, all of which grow in fields and along streams in the park.

The population of white-tailed deer in the park may be too large for the ecosystem to support.

The big brown bat is one of seven bat species that live in the park.

Most of the mammals in the park are small and include chipmunks, mice, foxes, raccoons, and opossums. Voles, squirrels, and woodchucks also live in the forests and fields. Bats roost in caves.

Rivers and wetlands are home to muskrats, beavers, and river otters. Beavers use mud and sticks to dam streams and to build lodges in ponds and lakes. The lodges keep the beavers safe from predators and provide a cozy place to raise a family.

Bald eagles like to nest in very high places.

Birds

About 250 species of birds live in the park. Several are powerful birds of prey. Once **endangered**, bald eagles now nest in the park's tall trees. They hunt small mammals and other prey along the rivers and in the wetlands. Many species of hawks also live in the park.

Songbirds include mourning doves, scarlet tanagers, and northern orioles. Crows, jays, and sparrows also live in the forests and fields. Most of these birds eat seeds or insects, which are easy to find.

Great blue herons were not seen in Cuyahoga Valley National Park until the 1980s. Today, there are several mating pairs. These wading birds catch fish in the rivers and streams. They stand very still in the water, watching for their prey. When a fish swims by, the heron snatches it in its long beak. Ducks, swans, and geese also swim in the park's many waterways.

Two great blue herons guard their nest in the park.

Amphibians and Reptiles

The park's waterways and wetlands are a great home for frogs. Visitors can often hear the bullfrog's deep croak or the high peeping of spring peepers. Salamanders, also amphibians, hide under leaves on the forest floor, where it is cool and damp.

Reptiles include several kinds of turtles, including snapping turtles. Water snakes lie on logs or glide through the grass near a stream.

There are no poisonous snakes in Cuyahoga Valley National Park.

Like other reptiles, turtles heat their bodies by soaking in the warmth of the sun.

Dragonflies such as the eastern pondhawk have delicate, see-through wings.

Fish and Insects

Many species of fish swim in the park's waterways. Rivers are full of steelhead trout and bullhead. Bass, crappies, and bluegills live in lakes and ponds. Fishing is a popular activity in the park.

The smallest animals in the park are insects and spiders. More than 50 different butterflies, plus dragonflies, bees, and ants, are found here. Many different spiders, such as wolf spiders and cave orb weavers, live in the park as well.

THE BIG TRUTH!

National Parks Field Guide: Cuyahoga Valley

Here are a few of the hundreds of fascinating animals you may see in the park.

Coyote

Scientific name: *Canis latrans*

Habitat: Grasslands, woods

Diet: Mice, squirrels, frogs, fish, fruit

Fact: Coyotes can run more than 40 miles (64 km) per hour.

Beaver

Scientific name: *Castor canadensis*

Habitat: Ponds, marshes, riverbanks

Diet: Tree bark, water plants

Fact: Beavers can build dams that are up to 10 feet (3 m) tall.

Indiana bat

Scientific name: *Myotis sodalis*

Habitat: Caves, woods

Diet: Insects

Fact: This bat is endangered.

Bald eagle

Scientific name: *Haliaeetus leucocephalus*

Habitat: Wetlands

Diet: Fish, reptiles, small mammals, birds

Fact: The bald eagle has been the symbol of the United States since 1782.

Northern water snake

Scientific name: *Nerodia sipedon*

Habitat: Lakes, ponds, rivers, streams

Diet: Fish, frogs, salamanders, worms

Fact: These harmless snakes look a lot like a venomous snake called the water moccasin.

Spotted salamander

Scientific name: *Ambystoma maculatum*

Habitat: Forests near rivers and streams

Diet: Insects, worms, spiders

Fact: Salamanders spend most of their time hiding underground or under leaves and rocks.

Wildflowers bloom along the Haskell Run Trail.

CHAPTER 4

An Abundance of Plants

With the park's forests, fields, and wetlands, a wide range of plants both big and small thrive in Cuyahoga Valley. Visitors hike through towering forests of **deciduous** and evergreen trees. Fields of wildflowers, blooming in an array of colors, brighten the park's spring days.

The park is home to more than 900 different species of plants.

Colorful Ground Cover

The park's grasses include Kentucky bluegrass and timothy. Wetter areas have tiny-flowered sedges. There is also an area of prairie grass, which was planted before the park was created. Its grasses are not native to Ohio.

Colorful wildflowers such as goldenrod, asters, trilliums, bluebells, and violets bloom in fields. Many grow in damp areas near creeks and other bodies of water. The moist air also helps mosses and ferns grow.

Plant Life of Cuhahoga Valley

Trees

A mix of deciduous and evergreen trees makes up the park's forests. Most are secondary growth forest. That means they were regrown after being cleared by people.

Hickory

Hemlock

Grasses and Wildflowers

Grasses and wildflowers abound in the park's open meadows. Wetlands and forest floors are also filled with greenery.

Kentucky Bluegrass

Asters

Mosses and Ferns

These green plants flourish in moist areas around water and on forest floors and trees. Some of these plants even cling to cliffs.

Moss and Lichen

Ferns

New Growth

Forests have grown in the Cuyahoga Valley for thousands of years. When farmers came in the 1800s, they cut down vast areas of forests to plant crops. After the National Park Service took over the land, new trees began to grow. Deciduous trees such as oak, beech, and hickory flourish. So do evergreens including pine, hemlock, and spruce. Elm and chestnut trees once grew here, too. But infections wiped them out throughout the park many years ago.

The park's deciduous trees turn brilliant shades of yellow, red, and orange in fall.

A Deadly Invasion

Adult gypsy moth

Gypsy moths are an **invasive species** that has caused enormous damage in the United States. They were first introduced in Massachusetts in the 1800s. Some of the insects accidentally escaped from a scientist's room. In the caterpillar phase of their life cycle, gypsy moths are exceptionally hungry. They can eat so much of a tree's leaves that the tree weakens and becomes prone to disease and parasites. Cuyahoga Valley experienced a huge gypsy moth infestation between 1996 and 2000. The worst year was 1999, when caterpillars damaged more than 4,000 acres (1,619 hectares) of park trees.

Gypsy moth caterpillars

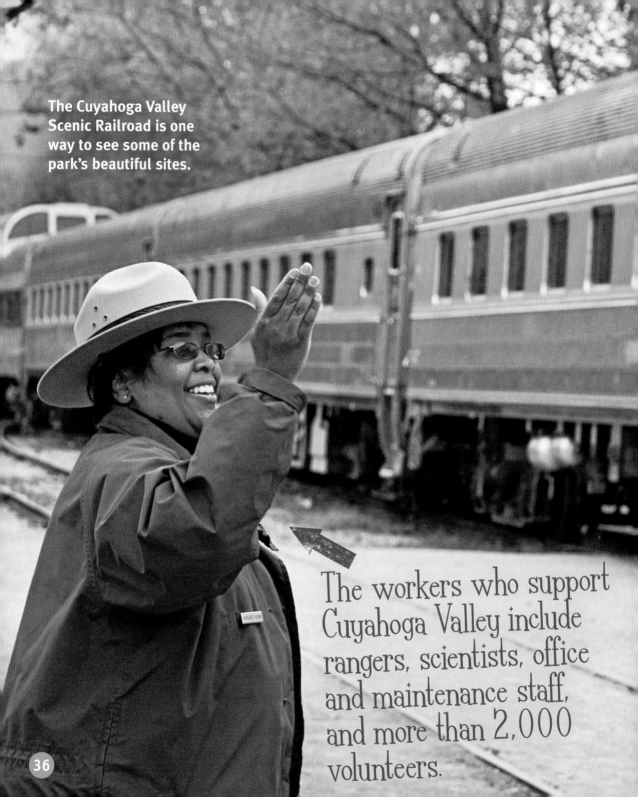

The Cuyahoga Valley Scenic Railroad is one way to see some of the park's beautiful sites.

The workers who support Cuyahoga Valley include rangers, scientists, office and maintenance staff, and more than 2,000 volunteers.

CHAPTER 5

Facing the Future

Like many natural habitats, Cuyahoga Valley faces challenges. Some of the most serious include invasive species and pollution. Invasive species such as the gypsy moth are dangerous because they can kill or crowd out native plants and animals. Programs are working to remove them.

The Cuyahoga River was once one of the most polluted rivers in the United States. People are working to clean the river so it is healthier for plants, animals, and humans. Park officials monitor, or study, water quality throughout the park every day. This helps identify problems.

Industries in Cleveland and other nearby cities create pollution that affects the surrounding region, including the park.

Pollution from the Skies

Park officials also monitor the park's air quality. Cuyahoga Valley is located between Cleveland and Akron, Ohio. These cities are major **industrial** centers. Air pollution from their factories spreads into the park and can harm plants and animals. Pollution also reduces visibility, making the park less enjoyable for visitors. Government officials are working to limit pollution from these industrial areas.

Direct Damage

Unfortunately, individuals sometimes also cause trouble in the park. They may leave trash, bother or harm animals, or damage plants.

Cuyahoga Valley National Park is a beautiful place. If you visit any national park, follow park rules. Ask a ranger for help if you have any questions or concerns. With work and respect, the Cuyahoga Valley's beauty will be enjoyed for many years to come. ★

Cuyahoga River was once scarred by trash (above). Today (right), it has a healthier natural habitat.

Map Mystery

A boardwalk offers a stunning view of this beautiful water feature at Cuyahoga Valley National Park. Follow the directions below to find it. What is the feature's name?

Directions

1. Start at the park's tallest waterfall, Brandywine Falls.

2. Hike west to find a railroad.

3. Take a scenic train ride north to Station Road Bridge.

4. Leave the train and head north until you find a house with a name that begins with the letter F.

5. Follow the border of the park north and then east. Look for a waterfall named after a piece of clothing worn for a special occasion.

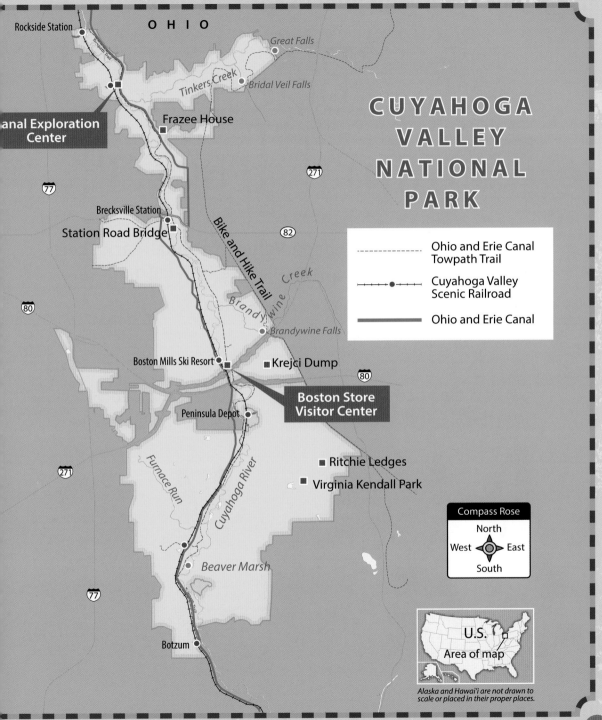

Rockside Station

O H I O

Great Falls

Tinkers Creek

Bridal Veil Falls

Canal Exploration Center

Frazee House

CUYAHOGA
VALLEY
NATIONAL
PARK

271

77

82

Brecksville Station

Station Road Bridge

Bike and Hike Trail

Brandywine Creek

- - - - - - - - Ohio and Erie Canal
Towpath Trail

━┿━┿━●━┿━┿━ Cuyahoga Valley
Scenic Railroad

━━━━━━━ Ohio and Erie Canal

80

Brandywine Falls

Boston Mills Ski Resort

Krejci Dump

80

Peninsula Depot

Boston Store
Visitor Center

271

Furnace Run

Cuyahoga River

Ritchie Ledges

Virginia Kendall Park

Compass Rose

North

West ◈ East

South

Beaver Marsh

77

Botzum

U.S.

Area of map

Alaska and Hawai'i are not drawn to
scale or placed in their proper places.

Be an Animal Tracker!

If you're ever in Cuyahoga Valley National Park, keep an eye out for these animal tracks. They'll help you know which animals are in the area.

Coyote

Paw length: 2.5 inches (6.4 cm)

White-tailed deer

Hoof length: 4 inches (10 cm)

River otter

Paw length: 3–4 inches (7.6–10.2 cm)

Beaver

Hind foot length: 6 inches (15.2 cm)

Raccoon

Paw length: 2–3 inches (5.1–7.6 cm)

Great blue heron

Foot length: 6–8 inches (15.2–20.3 cm)

True Statistics

Length of the Cuyahoga River in the park: 22 mi. (35 km)

Number of invasive plant species in the park: 16

Number of human-made lakes and ponds: More than 100

Number of mammal species: 39

Number of bird species: About 250

Number of fish species: More than 65

Number of reptile species: 20

Number of amphibian species: 19

Number of bat species: 7

Number of plant species: More than 900

Did you find the truth?

(F) The great blue heron disappeared from the park in the 1980s.

(T) Cuyahoga Valley was once at the bottom of the sea.

Resources

Books

Bailer, Darice. *What's Great About Ohio?* Minneapolis: Lerner Publications, 2016.

Flynn, Sarah Wassner, and Julie Beer. *National Parks Guide U.S.A.* Washington, DC: National Geographic, 2016.

Stille, Darlene. *Ohio*. New York: Children's Press, 2015.

Tornio, Stacy. *Ranger Rick: National Parks!* Guilford, CT: Muddy Boots Press, 2016.

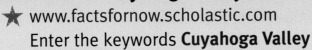

Visit this Scholastic website for more information on Cuyahoga Valley National Park:

★ www.factsfornow.scholastic.com
Enter the keywords **Cuyahoga Valley**

Important Words

canal (kuh-NAL) a channel that is dug across land so boats or ships can travel between two bodies of water

deciduous (dih-SIJ-oo-uhs) shedding all leaves every year in fall

endangered (en-DAYN-jurd) at risk of becoming extinct, usually because of human activity

fossils (FAH-suhlz) bones, shells, or other traces of animals or plants from millions of years ago, preserved as rock

glaciers (GLAY-shurz) slow-moving masses of ice formed when snow falls and does not melt because the temperature remains below freezing

industrial (in-DUHS-tree-uhl) of or having to do with factories and making things in large quantities

invasive species (in-VAY-sihv SPEE-sheez) plants or animals that enter a place in large numbers, usually with a negative effect on native species

mills (MIHLZ) buildings that contain machinery for grinding flour or producing other materials

sediment (SED-uh-muhnt) rock, sand, or dirt that has been carried to a place by water, wind, or a glacier

wetlands (WET-landz) land where there is a lot of moisture in the soil

Index

Page numbers in **bold** indicate illustrations.

amphibians, 26, **29**

bald eagles, **24, 29**
bats, 18, **23, 29**
Beaver Marsh, **17**
beavers, 10, 17, 23, **28, 43**
birds, 16, 17, **20**, 21, **24–25, 29, 43**
Brandywine Creek, 17
Brandywine Falls, **6**, 13, 17
Bridal Veil Falls, 40–41

coyotes, 22, **28, 42**
Cuyahoga River, 8, 9, 10, 11, **14, 16**, 37, **39**
Cuyahoga Valley Scenic Railroad, **16, 36**

deer, **22, 42**

establishment, 9, 12, 13

ferns, 32, **33**
fish, 9, 16, 25, 27
Ford, Gerald, **9**
fossils, 7
frogs, 16, 17, 26
fur trade, 8, 10

glaciers, 8, 18
grasses, 22, 32, **33**
great blue herons, **25, 43**
gypsy moths, **35**

Haskell Run Trail, **30**

insects, 16, 24, **27, 35**

Krejci Dump, **19**

maps, **7**, 40–**41**
mills, 11, **14**, 15
mosses, 17, **18**, 32, **33**

Native Americans, **8**, 9, 10

Ohio and Erie Canal, **9, 10**
otters, 23, **43**

peregrine falcons, **20**, 21
pollution, 19, 37, **38, 39**

raccoons, 23, **43**
railroads, **11**, 15, **16, 36**
reptiles, 16, **26, 29**
Ritchie Ledges, **18**

salamanders, 26, **29**
settlers, 8, 9, 10, 11, 15
shale, 7
snakes, 26, **29**
spiders, 27

timeline, **8–9**
Tinkers Creek, 16
tourism, **11, 13**, 15, 18, 19, 31, 38
trails, **13**, 15, 18, **30, 41**
trees, 17, **24**, 31, **33, 34**, 35

Virginia Kendall Park, 9, 12

waterfalls, **6**, 13, 17
wildflowers, **30**, 31, 32, **33**
workers, 19, **36**, 37, 38

About the Author

Joanne Mattern has written more than 250 books for children. She especially likes writing about all the amazing places on Planet Earth. Joanne also loves to write about animals, plants, and the natural world. She grew up in New York State and still lives there with her husband, four children, and several pets.